T0051286

Palimpsests

By the Same Author

Poetry Collections

Epiphanies
Rudiments of Grace
Home from Home
Lifelines
Beautiful Lofty Things
In Praise of the Shades
Heartlands
The Horn of Plenty
The Roman Centurion's Good Friday
South Africans
Mann Alive! Poems and Video
Kites
New Shades
A New Book of South African Verse in English
First Poems

Plays in Verse

The Ballad of Dirk de Bruin
Thuthula
Mahoon's Testimony
Walking on Gravity
Frail Care

Palimpsests

by

Chris Mann

DRYAD PRESS

People! Read Poetry

Palimpsests

Dryad Press (Pty) Ltd
Postnet Suite 281, Private Bag X16, Constantia, 7848,
Cape Town, South Africa
www.dryadpress.co.za/business@dryadpress.co.za

Copyright © poems Chris Mann
All rights reserved

No part of this book may be reproduced or transmitted in any form or by any
electronic or mechanical means, including photocopying and recording, or any
other information storage or retrieval system, without prior written permission
from the publisher or copyright holder

Cover design: Ben Grib
Typography: Stephen Symons
Editor: Michèle Betty
Copy Editor: Helena Janisch

Set in 9.5/14pt Palatino Linotype

First published in Cape Town by Dryad Press (Pty) Ltd, 2021

ISBN 978-1-990992-26-1 (Print)
ISBN 978-1-990992-27-8 (Electronic)

Visit **www.dryadpress.co.za** to read more about all our books and to buy
them. You will also find features, links to author interviews and news of author
events. Follow our social media platforms on Instagram and Facebook to be the
first to hear about our new releases.

The Shades are deep in our memory

~ Chris Mann

CONTENTS

Preface

Like many words in English, 'palimpsest' originates in ancient Greek: it conjures up a manuscript, written on parchment so precious that one text is rubbed out and replaced by another. Behind the most recent text lie the faint shadows of earlier thoughts, images, stories and desires – the textual ruins of previous civilisations, buried, like Atlantis, beneath the sea changes of history.

'Palimpsests' is an apt title for this collection of Chris Mann's intriguing and finely-wrought poems, which engage with these shadows to interrogate and comment on a contemporary world, in which, *inter alia*, materialism, disguised as 'progress', the mendacity of the political elite's rhetoric and the abuse of technology have resulted in the kind of moral bankruptcy that characterised the fall of past civilisations. Similarly, in the course of our frenzied 'getting and spending', we have indeed lain waste our powers and forgotten how to listen to old Triton blowing his horn.

Just as authors Freud and Camus turned to Greek mythology for their philosophies of the human predicament, so Chris Mann peoples his poems with characters from Greek and Roman mythology to reflect, for instance, on self-obsessed individualism, the nature of work in postmodern societies, the meaning of 'home' and the redemptive power of love and compassion: Narcissus, Sisyphus, Odysseus and Penelope, and Orpheus and Eurydice, are among the individuals and couples the reader meets, or is reminded of, in this collection.

The figure of Orpheus, both poet and seer, reminds us that what we know of Greek mythology is essentially what has been preserved in literature – for instance, in the epic poems of Homer, the lyric verse of Sappho, the odes of Pindar and the extant Greek tragedies. Chris Mann is fully aware of this and his careful research, which extends to Greek prose writers such as Plato, Thucydides and Plutarch's 'Life of Pericles', includes some important Roman sources as well. These sources range from Ovid's brilliant *Metamorphoses* (essential for the myth of Narcissus) to the love poems of Catullus, the teasing voices of Horace, and Tacitus's *Agricola*, in which Mann engages with one of the Roman historian's most daring inventions – a speech in which a British chieftain denounces Roman colonisation and its attendant atrocities.

Mann's allusive intertextuality and his appropriation of ancient myths and rituals are not confined to foundational texts in the history of Western literature. The 'Princess of Heaven' (*Inkosazana yeZulu*), the Zulu fertility goddess who presides over marriage, is 'Aphrodite's second cousin'; the clan bard Msebenzi Hlongwane is the 'Homer of the Drakensberg'; the vegetable offerings floating in Hlambeza Pool (reminiscent of Horace's fresh spring stained with a kid's blood) are offerings to the shades or ancestors who constitute the chain of being linking the living and the dead in African belief systems, just as a palimpsest connects the ancient world to the modern.

Chris Mann's *Palimpsests* restores lost civilisations to us and warns us of their fates. The colonisation of Africa began with colonies (like Utica) established by the Phoenicians and Greeks in North Africa. For the British chieftain, Roman colonisation was nothing but devastation dressed up as 'peace'. Yet, the agents of Roman imperialism, Christianised like their foes, became the Vandals' subservient victims, internalising the fears and despair they themselves spawned in the peoples they had conquered. Conquest, colonisation and urbanisation involve the rape of Nature; there can be no more powerful symbol of the effects of this abuse and subsequent climate change than Plato's lost city of Atlantis, reclaimed by the rising seas.

In the ancient epics, the journey across the seas began as the warrior's journey home after war; continued with the migrations of exiles and refugees to new homes; and then metamorphosed into the journey of the initiate into a new stage of life or the journey into the interior of the soul. For Chris Mann, the Ithaca of Homer and Constantine Cavafy, which gave the traveller his 'wonderful voyage', is found at home with his own Penelope, where he risks voyaging daily on the Internet, Homer's loom replaced by a mobile phone.

This image of the Odyssean voyage, grounded within the emotional security of a loving, familial relationship, contrasts with images of the loneliness of those, like Narcissus, severed from their communities by soulless obsessions. Through the use of an immediate narrative voice, both in monologues and dialogues, Mann personalises classical myths and history in his poems, constantly suggesting that without community and connectedness, memories fade as in palimpsests and sever the chain of being that links the living and the dead.

In a good example, Mann transforms prose accounts of the death-by-plague of the great Athenian statesman, Pericles, into a dramatic two-act poem reminiscent of Robert Browning: in the first, the man, who left a lasting memorial of his achievements on the Acropolis of Athens, dies in agony and is sent on his way to the underworld by his great love, Aspasia, who places the coin on his tongue to ensure the passage of his shade across the River Styx; in the second, set three years later, when the city of Athens is in the grip of yet another wave of the disease, more contagious than the first, Aspasia transmutes the pain of her memories and grief into a love song, accompanied on the harp. 'What's life if there's no love, what's love,' she sings, 'without a wisdom greater than the self?' Mann's Aspasia, as she crafts the past into poetry, reveals how creativity and art can heal, even in the midst of death and despair.

In *Palimpsests*, Chris Mann's poems demonstrate the kind of technical polish one might expect from a previous winner of the Newdigate Prize for Poetry at Oxford[1] and from an Honorary Professor of Poetry at Rhodes University. Experiments with metre and form, as well as the judicious use of an armoury of rhetorical effects, evidence a fine technical skill. In the following extract from Mann's 'Aphrodite's Southern Cousin', the eight-syllable line, the rise and fall of the iambic tetrameter, and the sibilance, assonance and enjambment combine to imitate the movements and sounds of the fish, the moths and the nightjar, and the breathing of the worn-out sleepers in the country town.

> On calm and tender summer nights,
> when fishes bite the wobbling moon,
> and moths fly up to silvery fruit,
> sprinkling the space among the boughs,
> the nightjar glides from sill to sill
> across the worn-out, sleeping town.

The mimetic lyricism of these lines, which must be read aloud to be appreciated, is in itself a kind of palimpsest, reminding us that classical Greek poetry and the myths it preserves were

---

1 In 1973. Other recipients include Matthew Arnold, Oscar Wilde, John Buchan and Alan Hollinghurst.

performed to the music of the lyre, and that the art of poetry is not simply emotion recollected in tranquillity, but hard work, aimed at communication and persuasion, carefully chiselled in the poet's workshop of words. Mann's 'The Statues on the Pier' encapsulates this well: referring to the empty plinths on the pier, the poet exhorts the reader, 'Cast your own compassion there in bronze. I give you the metal, I usher you into the foundry of your heart.'

Michael Lambert
Pietermaritzburg
June 2021

Heraclitan Heresies

I

So what if map and satellite
can fix your place in space and time?

For you and all you know are flux,
with water, fire and earth and air.

Listen: can you not hear the surf
grinding the coast of Greece to dust?

Watch: can you not see India's drift
slow-ram Tibet into the sky?

II

Lead me to the moral high ground
and I will climb the rainbow's arch.

Isolate the causes of war
and I'll nail down the shifting sea.

III

Is life not flux sinewed by strife?
Is strife not bonded in the whole

as stress binds opposites by day,
and sciamachy riddles night?

Save your breath. The abstract-minded
have made a God of Plato's forms

and cannot hear you on your beach
shouting Homer into a gale.

The Pool of Narcissus

He's on his hands and knees among the ferns,
staring at the face in the water.
The din of the city below the trees,
faint sounds of singing from the temple,
dwindle in the silence of the glade.

The afternoon sun is hot on his shoulders,
somewhere far off, deep in the forest,
a girl keeps calling out his name.
He goes on staring, staring into the pool.

It's been like this for months, for years even.
Two figures, half-hidden in the trees,
have both become, how shall I put it,
discretely anxious about their son.

Surely it wasn't like this in the past?
Hadn't they better consult an oracle?
Friends spoke highly of Tiresias,
although quite elderly now, and blind.

Perhaps that blundering enthusiast
Hephaestus was yet again to blame.
The lame god's latest is in his hand,
a marvel – a miniature bough of gold
crafted in the fire and smoke of his smithy.

This, surely, wouldn't turn out to be
as awful as the chariots and arrows,
the breastplates, helmets and swords,
being, after all, so visionary?

Narcissus sighs, twitches the twig,
rippling the placid sheen of the pool,
till deep down below its rim of stones,
an amphitheatre on a hill appears,
tier above tier of crowded seats
above a harbour, a shimmer of sea,
and on the stage, a line of dancers,
a singer plucking the strings of a lyre.

He stares for a while, sways a little,
then twitches again, this way and that,
till runners in a stadium emerge,
cheered on by excited spectators,
Heracles in armour, smeared with gore,
hacking at helmeted troops on a plain,
then gliding below the lily pads,
her arms stretched out in front of her,
her body white and marble-smooth –
a nymph with long black hair.

Heavens above! his mother whispers,
how much longer do we have to wait?
What if Narcissus grows up like this,
unable to drag himself back home?

A cloud floats silently over the glade,
a few warm drops splash on his back
as if the soft small voice of the girl
was still trying to gain his attention.

Narcissus stares on, and on, and on.

Aphrodite's Southern Cousin

The speckled bird as brown as dust
that roosts inside a bush by day,
hiding its head against the glare,
at midnight pecked against the pane,
and gently pecked, until I saw
the starlight glitter through its beak.

On calm and tender summer nights,
when fishes bite the wobbling moon,
and moths fly up to silvery fruit,
sprinkling the space among the boughs,
the nightjar glides from sill to sill
across the worn-out, sleeping town.

It shook the sandman from my sight,
and when the tar-bound slopes had turned
to bush and rocky hill it sang,
There is a grass house in the hills,
above the coast where sugar spumes,
and lilies sprout, and no storms fly.

There, the Princess of the Heavens,
beside her dark-as-honey feet,
gathers up the dreams that reach her
and, stooping to her woven pots,
rinses them in rainbow water,
and stores them with the morning mist.

Go, waking sleeper, call to her,
and wading through the icy stream
in which the golden pebbles shine,
ask her if her power is love,
for she is old as she is young,
and without her, no one dreams.

I saw her then, beneath a tree
on which a crown of crimson burned,
and then the hill began to dim,
and standing in the greying rocks,
I heard the nightjar fade, from sill
to sill, across the windowed town.

The City of Atlantis in a Diver's Mask

If you should dream of diving off the coast of Greece,
make sure you see, riding the swells, the grey-white gull
that tried to guide head-strong Odysseus through a storm.

Don't miss the rusted hulks of ships below the waves,
the big-clawed crabs, the flit-by shimmer of the fish,
the coral's slow red shout of life inside the gloom,

then kicking slowly, swim on down the rocky slope
till in the wavering, dim blue underworld below
you see the marks of streets and houses on a plain.

Is Plato's myth, you think, *a figment of the mind*?
De-mist your face mask's glass, check belt and dials,
expel more bubbles from your harnessed buoyancy,

then free-fall head first through the circling sharks
until you see cracked urns, bronze dishes on the sand,
then turn, and flipper quietly down the silent street.

You'll turn and float inside a door, longing to greet
inside the airless rooms that gel their absences
a dark-haired man and wife, a child stroking a cat.

Gliding onwards past roofless stalls, dim colonnades
and vacant squares, you'll think, *God, what a tragedy!*
But why, why? Kicking up above a sea-mossed wall,

you'll drift across the cattle pens, the tanners' yards,
the charcoal burners' pits, the hovels round the gate,
the sheds along the quay, all still intact and joined.

It's then I think a dense, unknowing cloud of sand,
billowing with the surging tide, will smother you
till vision slowly shapes out of its swirl of grains.

A blur of grass, a field will bloom, and sailing up
and shining by like wisps of meadow thistledown,
the laughs of children playing among the asphodels.

Then shouts from town, the raucous bellow of a horn,
people running wildly, down streets and alleyways,
an old man hobbling fast across the market square,

the high priest lighting incense on the temple steps,
sheep on the trot, pigeon-flutters over courtyards,
the moneychangers tying bags below their robes,

and near a statue on a plinth, a woman being pulled
up onto the crowded porch-roof of the courthouse,
as ankle-, waist-, then chest-deep water in the streets

engulfs the banquet frescoed round a villa's hall,
and silent as the workings of the unforeseen,
a rising sheen of water floods the wooded plain.

You'll panic then, frantic to help, to warn people,
filling air sacs, will rise quickly, far too quickly,
gasping, giddy, tearing at the tendrils of weed

that, slithery, thick and writhing in the visor glass,
wrap clinging round your throat and breathing gear
a talisman of raped Medusa's endless outcast rage.

Breaching at last the lucent watery ceiling glass,
you'll swim your aqualung out of that underworld
and panting, nauseous, clamber back onto the boat.

Rest, rest, you'll say, as suddenly the sea mew fades
and bird specks sail like migrant souls above the bay,
the gently heaving, blue-pearl iridescence of the sea.

You'll see the smudgy skies of Athens down the coast,
a wind farm's slender spires above an olive grove,
the yachts, hotels, the flash of passing cars below,

then lifted sky-high by a landward-speeding swell,
will feel fierce pangs of caritas and jolts of dread
and wake – your wetsuit sweat, the sea a tousled bed.

The Curse of Sisyphus

I stood and stared across the cavern of a city's underground.
  Great multitudes of people were hurrying from the trains
and rising on the stairs towards the shops and office blocks.

I thought then of the shirt-sleeved traders in a stock exchange.
  Hunched up in tier on tier of desks, bargaining on their phones,
they stare as if entranced at graphs like jagged hills on screens.

I scanned my memories. A sweating man shaped into view,
  his back against a rock, shoving it up a hillside by the sea.
Is there no rest, I said to him, *no respite from such toil?*

He paused, the muscles of a straining thigh clenched in the sun.
  No, no respite, he said. *Work empties out and spins the man
who spurns the gods for gold and fame, for trinkets from a stall.*

*His soul shrinks to a whirling vacancy. The more he works,
  the more he strives to feed its appetites, the more he whirls –
far too busy to stop and pray, to dance, or weep, or sing.*

He gave a groan, then rubbed a calloused palm across his face.
  Without prayer, he said, *there is no rest, no music in the dark.
Look, look at me, you vortex heads, and pray your soul alive.*

Below the hill, the seals of Corinth basked beside the sea.
  The asphodels were out. His son ran laughing to a stream.
He shut his eyes and shoved again, and laboured on alone.

The Clan Bard of the Drakensberg

~ in memoriam Msebenzi Hlongwane, the praise poet of the
AmaNgwane clan

Behind that weathered face of yours,
a face that held a Grecian statue's look
of gaunt contempt at all things mean,

what memories of glossy cattle herds,
of honey-coloured domes of grass
and iron-bright spear blades seethed?

You came to me again, grey bard,
blind as a Homer of the Drakensberg
as I sat hot and fretful in my car,

clamped in a Midrand traffic crawl,
sending messages from my phone
to meetings streets and streets away.

Why had you come to haunt me there?
Knobbed stick, short spear in hand,
you flickered in my trafficked mind.

I wondered what you'd make of us,
you who'd strolled the hills barefoot,
breath-close to kin, to dung and dust.

How would you view the billboard ads,
the maze of streets, the rush, rush, rush
of symbiotic strangers round a town?

I turned a talk show's chatter down
and saw you whole, a frail old man
dressed in a ragged shirt and coat

shuffling over the dawn-brimmed dew
towards a cattle byre below the crags
where I had come to drink your springs.

On goat-scoured hills lies your pastoral epic
of thick-packed shacks, a shop, a school
and kin whose children wake in towns.

Is this what cities do to clans?
you made me ask as you trudged past
a rib-rack whippet suckling pups.

A pregnant girl yawned in a door,
a radio throbbed with gospel choirs
as you stretched out a hand and touched

a fence that kraaled a few thin cows,
turned to the sun, raised up a spear
and chanted out an orison of praise.

Still tense, at being so late, so stuck
inside a grid of trucks and cars,
I only heard faint remnants of your poem;

that phrase where one king's called
The-Morning-Star-who's-only-seen
by-those-who-get-up-with-the-dawn;

those references to pumpkin plants,
to fords and feuds now as obscure
as pot chips dug from cave-bed soil;

that warrior boast, dying in the air,
that Matiwane, your Hercules, slew
and slew until his eyes turned red.

Aaah Tshani! Grain-pit-of-memories!
Poet-whose-footsteps-the-dew-reveals!
You looked so small, yet so defiant

below that huge amphitheatre of rock.
How I admired and loved you then.
You prompt me still, my bardic shade,

to lift my voice, to praise the dawn
when I sit still and start to write
within the amphitheatre of a screen.

The Comrades Marathon

~ *after Pindar's Olympian odes and*
in memoriam Victor Clapham

Well Vic, I wonder what you'd make of this?
I mean the flag-hung square, the jostling crowds,
   a helicopter clattering through the dark,
runners in their thousands, massed down the street,
   and someone famous being interviewed
in a bright white glare on the steps of City Hall.

I wish you could be here, right here with us,
dressed in your baggy shorts and tennis shoes,
   smelling the wintergreen, the nervous sweat
and feeling strange pricklings in your skin
   as speakers boom the anthem down the street
that lifts the day from normal into epic time.

Isn't it much, much bigger than you thought?
At times I've wondered what you dreamed
   when, back home from the war to end all wars,
you'd sit in the hot steel cab of your train,
   swabbing your neck and chest with cotton waste
and slowly swigging a bottle of cold sweet tea.

Well Vic, each year, out of that dream emerge
not just the rugby types you started with,
   that group of balding friends in boxing vests
trotting off down a farm road with a laugh,
   but men and women of all sorts and shapes,
the black, the blonde, the bronze of our humanity.

Does hope, a marathon of hope like this,
you make me ask, remind the heart of grace?
    Look, Vic, at what you got going with pride,
a huge, jostling ritual of human decency
    whose athletes set off down a cheering street
then toil across the troubled landscape of South Africa.

A Picnic Beside Hlambeza Pool

The pool is as you'd imagine it to be:
brown and narrow, mirroring cycads
and ferns, the crags of a deep ravine.
Spined succulents thicket the banks,
the pleated rocks and surface shales.

And we are as you might picture us,
sprawled on rugs with thermos flasks,
discussing new software and hardware,
exchanging stories of burnout, stress,
armed robbery and patients with AIDS.

A green cathedral, chirps someone,
smacking at horseflies and midges.
The children pick through the rushes
and clambering onto adult shoulders
dive off into the water with shrieks.

Hey, what's this? Bobbing on the edge,
roofed in by naves of ferns and reeds,
three fist-sized crumplings of paper,
pumpkin seeds in the boat of the one,
white beads and tobacco in the others.

Offerings, says a friend, *you know,
like Greeks and Romans used to make.
Not to gods, to the people of the river,
the ancestors who Xhosa locals claim
are intercessors, their links with God.*

Perhaps we shouldn't have swum here.
The words reverberated across a silence.
I felt the cycad fronding of the unknown
breaking out around and inside us again,
and glimpsed, deep in a pool of memory,

the faces of the living dead, the shades.

In Praise of the Shades

Hitching across a dusty plain one June,
down on one of those dead-straight backveld roads,
I met a man with rolled-up khaki sleeves
who told me his faults and then his beliefs.
It's amazing that some people discuss
even more with hitch-hikers than their friends.

His bakkie rattled a lot on the ruts
so I'm not exactly sure what he said.
Anyway, when he'd talked about his church
and when the world had changed from mealie stalks
to sunflowers, which still looked green and firm,
he lowered his voice, and spoke about his shades.

This meant respect I think, not secrecy.
He said he'd always asked them to guide him,
and that, even in the city, they did.
He seemed to me a gentle, balanced man,
and I was sorry to stick my kit-bag
onto the road again and say goodbye.

When you are alone and brooding deeply,
do your teachers and loved ones desert you?
Stand on a road when the fence is whistling.
You say, *It's the wind,* and if the dust swirls,
The wind again, though you never see it.
The shades work like the wind, invisibly.

And they have always been our companions,
dressed in the flesh of the children they reared,
gossiping away from the books they wrote,
a throng who even in the strongest light
are whispering, *You are not what you are,*
remember us, then try to understand.

They come like pilgrims from the hazy seas
that shimmer at the borders of a dream –
not such spirits that they can't be scolded,
not such mortals that they can be profaned,
for scolding them, we honour each other,
and honouring them, we perceive ourselves.

When all I seem to hear about these days
is violence, injustice and despair,
or humourless theories, from cynical hearts,
to rescue us all from our human plight,
those moments in a bakkie on a plain
make sunflowers from a waterless world.

The Statues on the Pier

~ Port Alfred pier, Eastern Cape, South Africa

A cold wind, buffeting in across a blank desolation of sea.
  Terns flung into the air, veils of sand flying down a beach.
And bolted onto the open-air gallery of a pier, the statues.

They're larger than life, but not beyond its flesh and blood.
  Their backs are turned, away from the torn sky and the sea.
With metalled eyeballs they stare at their habitat – the land.

The hand of one is raised, breaking stone in a prison quarry.
  The women of the next, rimed with salt, cradle a child.
Chiselled in the barnacled plinth of a third: *Love one another.*

Other plinths stand vacant on the pier. Can you not see them?
  They're yours to fill. Cast your own compassion there in bronze.
I give you the metal, I usher you into the foundry of your heart.

A wave smashes against the rocks, the air whitens with spray.
  It cataracts down flared nostrils, the muscle of backs, a thigh.
Empty plinths gleam in the sun. Place your own shades there now.

Epiphanies

Whoever grew wise
without sorrow?

Whoever loved
until they'd trusted
enough to bleed?

And who understood
until they'd shivered
in terror at their ignorance?

The Ithaca of the Internet

Some find it laughable that I should still love words,
  should eat as bread the poetry of prayers and songs
and mutter on for hours to metaphor a dream
  when language, to their world, means data, list and tweet.

Like them, I hanker for new sights, and sail each day
  out of a desktop port as if into an old Greek poem
where lotus-lands of images waylay my ship
  and sailors like Odysseus lie drugged on perfumed sheets.

My hungry soul, like his, is tugged back as it sails
  towards the salt and bread of distant memories,
the talking, hurts and cares, the laughter, hugs and tears
  inked in the logos-land, the Ithaca of home.

Hello! I turn and see her waving at me from the stoep,
  she's talking to our son and treats me to a smile,
a love-shone smile that drops my sails flat on the deck:
  Penelope anew, afresh, her loom a mobile phone.

Living with Eurydice

I leaned across the fence at home
and looked out at the field
where you and I had walked at ease
so many times before.

A wind came speeding out the heat
and blew into my face.
It carried hints of gums in bloom,
hot soil and far off rain.

My netherworld of memories
released a flux of ghosts.
You came and went then in my mind,
a wash, a twitch of light

who played a kite, ran with a child,
and gazed up at the moon.
You changed so fast I shut my eyes
to catch your fleeting wraith.

Sounds of barking, thoughts in flurries
came breaking, rushing through.
I focussed darkness. Of you thought.
Waited. Glimpsed, then lost you.

I tried again. In darkness, calm.
At last. In flickers, blurs.
You in your jeans. Crouching. Laughing.
.Barefoot. Frisbee in hand.

Feinting, darting, this way and that
across the evening field,
laughing, calling, crouching forward,
your shirtsleeves all pushed up,

about to send your joy at being there
skimming across the rain,
the bright rain of a summer shower
to me who longed for you

this side the chasm of past time.

Sapphic Fragments

Hands

Your hands, the slim fingers,
the nails tapering like almonds,
the risen moons at the quick –

I watch them at the table,
smoothing out an invoice,
texting a friend overseas,

sitting a child on your lap,
buttering a slice of bread,
stretching out for grace.

They seem so subtle,
so naked and precise
I cannot wait for night to fall.

Jeans

Morning spring-shine,
windows, opened,
a rumpled bed.

Your sunlit jeans
lay on the floor,
the zip gleaming

as if the rungs
of Jacob's ladder
were also there.

Metamorphoses on Waking

You stand at the foot of the bed,
naked to the waist, face
still drowsy in the morning sun.

Shaking the hair from your eyes,
you put on a filigree of clothing,
perching your doves in its lace.

You look so potent, so womanly,
a sculpture, an archetype,
an Aphrodite in a leaf-green bra.

I sit up in bed, arms outstretched.
You smile and shake your head.
No, not now, you say, *I'm late.*

Next thing, your blouse is on,
you've bent, kissed my cheek,
grabbed your things and gone.

But all the molecules of me,
like dust motes in a sunbeam,
have come alight and dance.

The Seahorse Pegasus

I saw you first behind thick glass.
A horsehead in a sea-grass forest,
a spiral of tail curled round a stem.

The short stubby fin on your back
began to undulate its fan-thin ribs.
You flew slowly through your air.

You reminded me then of Pegasus;
of catfish and whiskered molluscs
in the salt marshes of your lagoon;

of Ovid's mind, where vegetation,
people, animals and deities merge
in the estuarine tides of mythic time.

I pressed my forehead to the glass.
Your green had an octopus mottle.
Your eye-glance was all chameleon.

Nearby, a sprinkle of infants hung,
as spindly as plankton mosquitoes.
You'd reared their eggs in a pouch,

a kangaroo womb until their birth.
Are you creation's perfect male?
A sea-mare floated from a reed,

your partner, your spouse for life.
I wondered if she knew emotion
and felt what we suppose is love.

The bone-hoops beneath her skin
gave her a crinoline, bridal look.
Your daily wedding dance began.

She glided down an aisle of pillars,
entwined her curl of a tail in yours
and rose slowly, twirling with you

within a watery tabernacle of life.

The Fall of Thrasybulus the Tyrant

Chronos or *kairos* – take your pick:
Syracuse, the harbour, a blazing hot day,
my master's sailing ship tied to the quay,
me bundling papyrus reeds into sheaves
while keeping an eye on the cargo on deck,
the dockhands lounging around a fountain,
hustling for a job, a crust of bread –
some sprawled in the shade of cypress trees,
sick, poor wretches, with some new disease.

Across the flagstones rose the colonnades,
the stalls and temples of the city square,
so close I could hear the hubbub of a crowd
and the voice of a speaker on Athena's steps
could see the graffiti charcoaled on walls,
the rope looped round a statue's neck.

What's new, I thought, *the wine of adulation
becomes in the end the vinegar of contempt.
Down with Thrasybulus!* the crowd shouted,
the rope tightened, the statue tilted forward,
then toppled with a crash to the ground.

My master, his face sweating, paunch bouncing,
came running from the melee in the square
past anxious old men, being led in a group
towards the porch of the magistrates' court,
and sullen roughnecks, gathering on a bridge,
some casually hitting bronze dryads with staves.

Pompous oaf, what mayhem he's caused,
my master snorted as he reached the quay.
Hoist the sails, things are going to improve,
for traders, migrants, even slaves, my Ethiop.

I've heard that before, I thought to myself
as leaping on board he bellowed at the crew,
Athens, Athens here we come!

The Plague of Athens (430–426 BCE)

I

The Death of Pericles

An autumn's equinox, the night air hot and still,
   a full moon, high above the rooftops, trees and streets,
shapes out a chalk-pale palimpsest of mythic time:
   the marble columns of a temple built on rock,
a rugged coast, the silence of a calm and silvered sea.

The sad-eyed drinkers in a bar have staggered home,
   the sage who'd argued Eros off his ivied plinth
and broached a woman seer's thoughts – that love's desire
   torments the soul until it seeks transcendent truth –
ponders the glisten of a snail track on a shadowed wall.

Hush now, this is sleep's pause, the waking hour
   when thoughts and dreams, as if uplifted by the swells,
the pulse and heave of shoreward surging swells,
   glimmer a midnight city in a cove of rocks,
then dark out in the mind-brain's earth-whirled sea.

Look, isn't that grunting night gown on a bed
   a temple clerk, totting up wages, grants and fees,
the unpaid levies of a league of sea-edged states?
   And there, a pearl-pale murmuring still half asleep,
isn't that lithe Aspasia crafting a phrase for Pericles?

I wouldn't be a wandering Orpheus of the Internet,
    a fan of rhythmic Homer's word-strung lyre,
were I to hide behind a screen of slatted prose
    the quiet radiance of the moonlight in that room,
the unseen resonance that brings to life a dream, a song.

Here then's a gleam of leather armour by a bed,
    the rippled ivory of a tousled linen sheet,
an inked reed-nib, a black and ochre water jug
    around whose clay gymnasium dim figures run,
and on a sill, the moonlit frame and string-set of a harp.

Hush now and let this be, for Pericles has stirred,
    the sweat-gleamed torso on the bed – the orator,
the energising nexus of a politics, a fleet,
    public works, art, a hundred city states – has coughed,
and sitting up, Aspasia has shrieked, *Oh no, not more!*

Water! he gasps, *my head's on fire, my body burns!*
    He yanks the sheet aside, shudders, twists over
then retches a foul-smelling vomit on the tiles,
    foul as the rotting kelp and fish strewn on a beach
after a storm has roiled and moiled the silt beds of a shore.

Aspasia, kneeling, helps him roll back on the bed.
    Don't touch! he yells, swears, gabbles gibberish, slumps,
his face livid, his breath foetid, his eyes blood-red and dulled
    as if a tide had turned the plankton-seethe of plans
inside his soldier-statesman's brain into a bruise-red sludge.

Hush now and let Aspasia's wailing wake the streets
   and rouse the watchman dozing on the city walls,
bring into frame her hands as she wipes clean his face,
   strokes shut his staring eyes then places on his tongue
a coin for his migration to that substrate of space-time,

   the hum of energy that holograms the underworld.

II

The Love Song of Aspasia

O Pericles, you'd hate to see great Athens now,
   the streets empty, the best physicians dead,
the marketplace a morgue of shuttered stalls.

It's three years on, the clouds beyond the sill
   scud slowly past the moon like refugees
shouldering sacks and trudging to oblivion.

Down at the docks, the quays are desolate,
   the wine for Syria sours in the heat
and weevils waste the sheds of Egypt's grain.

The city's refuse carts stand in their yard,
   there's sewage, rats and flies in every square
and beds and bodies smouldering on pyres.

It's all so hideous, and so terrifying!
   Your aunt before she died told visitors
the cause is in the very air we breathe,

the foul miasma that the swamps and mist,
   the stick-and-canvas hovels of the poor,
the surly slaves and immigrants exhaled.

Not so, that playwright friend of yours replied,
   It's punishment – Athenians have become
so rich and arrogant they've made the gods

the gilded conscripts of their own desires.
   Beware the messenger, the Proteus-imp
who stalks with death the hubris of mankind.

He's wrong, he never understood how much
   recovery from conquest was your mount –
and people's votes, not luxury, your spur.

I watched you snub the banquets and the bribes
   and richly fund the warships and the city walls,
the athletes, scholars, singers, roads and drains –

not just that bronze colossus on a hill
   flaunting a spear higher than the temple
in which her ivory double's robed in gold.

Ah Pericles, what of Athena now?
   This thing is back – it paused and now it's back
more pitiless, more ravenous than before.

What of the stern-eyed, jewelled paragon
   of warfare's triumph when there's such hunger,
such chaos and despair in Athens now?

Whispering at the door, the scarf-wrapped heads
   back off when I get up and slowly creep
towards the harp still on our sill's dim shrine.

Oh, Pericles, it's three years on tonight,
   I find it hard to weep, still can't believe
I'll never hold you in my arms again

or see you on a platform shape in speech
   the vision of the Athens that you sought
or walk with sculptors round the building sites.

How much I wish I were Penelope
   who knew her mariner would turn for home!
But let the harp you loved replace her loom.

You said to me Pythagoras had proved
   geometry's in the humming of a string
and music in the space between the spheres.

So let me lean across the shadowed sill,
   my taut-strung craft in both my hands,
and turn from silent marble on a rock

towards the distant glimmer of the sea
   and throb by throb, fly out into the night
a love song like a bird in search of you.

Oh, Pericles, can't you, don't you hear me?
   What's life if there's no love, what's love
without a wisdom greater than the self?

Grim tyrants may restore their grip of iron,
  rampaging Spartans burn the marketplace,
barbarians leave the Parthenon in ruins

but there's a permanence in love's desire
  as strange and lovely as a throbbing string.
Oh Pericles, can't you, don't you hear me?

Scapegoat

~ Nicodemus of Alexandria, a wool merchant living in Athens,
to city officials before the annual pharmakos (purification) ritual

I can take it when you bad-mouth me for doing something wrong –
 can take it when you say you think some people don't belong.
But ousting me won't bring more jobs or cure low self-esteem,
 the burning and the looting start within that twisted dream.

I've watched so many blame-artists switch targets down the years;
 it starts way back when we're still young, the teasing and the jeers.
If you think oth'ring gets things right, well – have another go;
 I've watched it make extortion, rape and brib'ry grow and grow.

It's not that I walk past the pain the poorest locals feel;
 it's just that dumping stuff on me won't help the city heal.
Who's ever cleansed a marketplace of sleaze and avarice?
 You're mad to think I'll bear your sins into the wilderness.

This scapegoating's a cover-up, a scam you know can't last.
 Next week, your envy's bile will once again spew up the past.
Why don't you try a little love, and treat me like a friend?
 A rabid dog knows more of peace than spite that doesn't end.

There're Syrians in the bankers' stalls, new money being made.
 Why scowl at foreigners in bars? You've always lived off trade.
It's time you let Athena shush the doom-gods in your head.
 Don't sulk at work, don't booze and brood, then vent on me instead.

I see it now – a shrinking Greece of migrant loves and hates,
the longing for the road that leads towards Arcadia's gates.
The world's a place of broken dreams, just as it was before,
Well, I don't think I want to be a scapegoat anymore.

Saturnalia Satirica

satires wearing different masks

I

Truth

after Catullus

Why are the nicest girls so plain?
Don't laugh. Now that liberty
has turned to licence in Rome,
I can't think of a single woman
who's both virtuous and beautiful.

Worse still, those brutes, the men –
they make me sick. Even senators
with good looks, adorable wives,
farms in Umbria, Caesar's affection,
play fast and loose with the truth.

Let the love-crazed poets versify
the shapely white necks of swans,
persuading rich widows that theirs,
theirs is the best, the truest of arts
for being so charming, so beautiful.

That's Plato's heady twaddle.
Ha! The sow with hairy breasts
butting her piglets in a bog
is prettier by far than the swan
that paddles a politician's pond.

Pigs! Isn't the filthiest old boar
tusking up muck in dung-heaps
more honest than a rhetorician?
What truth's a poet's glacéd fig
when offal festers in the Forum?

No, the truth is me, Catullus,
me whom moneymen threaten
and adulterers malign and sue.
Stuff them. The fairest of poems
tell the ugliest of truths.

II

Perfect Sex

after Ovid

Don't shirk the shapeshifter that lurks
  inside the human genome's walls,
that burns inside a lecher's blood,
  a looting soldier's balls.

If sex and power best evolve
  survival for Charles Darwin's ape,
is perfect sex, for loveless men,
  not that vile thing, a rape?

III

On Philo's Move to Rome

after Martial

Philo's joined the scuttling, rat-brained rabble
  who flee the whole foul African affair,
and then, throughout their emigrant babble,
  exploit the colony they couldn't bear.

IV

Vanity

after Horace

And now, what's the matter, Demetrius?
  Huddled on a bench, picking at a sandal
and gazing gloomily over smoggy Rome,
  you look as miserable as one of your friezes –

one of the better ones, to tell the truth.
  A cypress, sooty; a Venus, vandalised ...
you couldn't have composed it better.
  I'd call it, *Ah woe is me, sans nymphs.*

Has someone bust their best Greek chisel,
  or chipped the tip off Cupid's perfect nose?
I bet that's what you'd tell me if I asked,
  but no, I won't, you look too forbidding.

I know, I know, you're not like that at all.
   You're sensitive, and intelligent, and kind,
and only look depressed and dourly grim
   because your patron was seen with a rival.

How you must hate him. The young poseur,
   all surface without any *gravitas,* you said,
dashing off frescoes for the *nouveau riche*
   as if tragedy and the gods had disappeared.

What a life – grovelling for commissions,
   riddled with envy, doubt and despair,
and chip, chip, chipping, year after year,
   at busts of scroungers and thug politicians.

Quite frankly, I could murder your tutor,
   who said you had *such hidden potential.*
Remember? The disaster began with flattery.
   He needed more pupils. Vanity did the rest.

Go and sell onions, start a whore house,
   emigrate to the wilds of barbarous Britain –
do anything, Demetrius, except more art!
   Why foist your misery on us till you die?

Listen, the toga on your latest Caesar
   still looks like a sack. Stop fleeing the truth!
Your appetite for fame will always exceed
   the impeccable mediocrity of your gifts.

V

Abstract Art

after Juvenal

I looked across the gallery.
Schoolkids were snickering
around a glassed display.
It's abstract art, now shush!
I heard a harassed teacher say.

Am I a mystifier of art
and art's great dream of life
to claim she hadn't erred?
Uplifted on a spike,
a rhino's dried-up, varnished turd.

VI

Priapus

after Horace

Imagine a banquet in a villa with a roaring fire
  when all the hills of Rome are white with snow.
I lay on my side, drowsed by the dark red wine,
  as silver-tongued Maecenas clapped his hands.

Three dancers came tripping through an arch,
  curtsied, smiled, then slowly raised their arms.
Their eyes were immodestly edged with black,
  the bangles on their ankles jingled and gleamed.

Libidius, one perfumed hand below his head,
  the other still clutching his newest playscript,
whispered, *I've been so depressed, Horatius,*
  but, thank the gods, love makes things new.

Ha! I thought to myself, don't make me laugh.
  A lecherous ape knows more of love than you.
Whose secret bedroom's a chamber of mirrors
  where courtesans come to pleasure his nights?

The dancers ran, leapt and spun on their toes,
  knelt down, threw back their long black hair
and undulated in ways that make men mad.
  Bavius dribbled duck soup on his paunch.

Libidius, at the end, staggered up on his feet,
  and muttering, *Ish marvellous, jus' marvellous!*
lunged at the breasts of the giggling Claudia
  who pulled him stumbling through an arch.

Maecenas clapped, the Syrian envoy cheered,
  and even the newest of his flattering parasites
oozed out a drunken *Ho, ho, ho!* and warbled
  in that atrocious Carthaginian accent of his.

Ha, cruel Venus, why do you still deceive us?
  Why do drunkards stumble down dark passages
knowing that at the end of the novelty awaits
  a lonelier, emptier desolation than before?

I stood, and wrapping my countryman's cloak
  around the indigestion growling in my bowels,
walked in the frozen garden to clear my head
  and saw brave Priapus on a plinth in the sleet.

Poor fellow, his huge, ridiculous manhood
  sticking out from under his wooden jerkin,
had no place to shelter from the icy blasts.
  He seemed such an idiot, so horribly alone.

I shivered, and crunching down the frosted path,
  could have sworn I heard behind black shutters
the shrieks of a nymph feigning consummation
  while a goat-legged satyr groaned on and on.

Well, what of it. Libidius will be back in spring,
  fleeing his wrinkles, and the rage of his wife,
as he tightens his belly on a garden bench
  and dandles a pretty new Claudia on his lap.

Behind them, Priapus, now cleaned and oiled,
  will gaze with hauteur from his marble plinth,
a scarecrow from the farms – now deemed a god!
  But what of it? To each his own delusions and pain.

Getting Ready for the Vandals

Should it ever be announced in the Forum
that the Vandals have landed on the coast
and are making their way to Rome,
ignore the panic in the speeches of the Senators,
the pale-faced crowds running through the streets
and the croak of the ravens above the temple of Jupiter.

Hurry straight home and tell your sons
to strap the panniers in the stables onto the mules,
conceal the family valuables under old sacking
and head for Tuscany, hooded like priests, as planned.

By now you'll have heard a lot about them,
the Vandals I mean, how they'd crossed from Spain
and like a cloud of locusts darkening the sky
had dropped with a pitiless whirr of wings
and stripped the farmlands and cities of Africa
of wheat and olives, fine linen, pottery and gold.

You'll also by now be concerned, deeply concerned
about the breakup of the tax-starved Empire
into feuding clans and belligerent alliances
administered by what a friend had ridiculed
as *small-minded opportunists* and *rapacious thugs*,
and will, discretely, have placed your savings
with relatives in Milan and friends in Greece
and decided to move to the countryside.

A modest dwelling, tucked in the mountains,
and not too costly, is what you had in mind,
with a view of vineyards, a vegetable garden,

and a marbled Venus on an ivied plinth
to assure your wife and adorable grandchildren
that love still had a place in the world.
And then, to remedy the sleepless nights
when age and foreboding anguish the mind,
the sight of calm grey wraiths of mist
drifting across a riverside meadow at dawn
like indistinct visitants from Elysian fields.

By now, of course, you'll have heard the rumours
concerning the tactics of their campaign,
how ragged men in a great country villa
would announce that they now owned the farm,
how they'd jump on a merchant's belly in town
and shout, *You lying bastard, bring out the rest!*
how they'd shove a woman face down on a floor
and with a fervour you find quite inexplicable,
would rape her in turns, cheered on by friends.

The Vandals had thus in a way become part of you,
had encouraged you to hire, at some expense,
mercenaries to guard your warehouse and home
and builders to increase the height of your walls
and gouge out a hideout below your floors.

Your wife by now will be hunched in its gloom,
the servants handing down amphorae of water,
your daughter, wide-eyed, hugging a doll,
as the din of the hawkers and oxcarts faded
and a silence, a stillness spread through the streets
as eerie as that before a thunderstorm
when bruise-dark clouds above the Capitol
would seethe like the robes of an angry Mars,

ready to rip the heavens with lightning
and the hearts of the citizens of Rome with fear.
You drag a paving stone over upturned faces,
then fling wide the shutters, doors and gates,
scatter rugs and brassware across the courtyard,
and once in the stables, climb into the rafters
and, on a small platform nailed over the beams,
sit small behind a pile of baled hay
and wait for the house-to-house search to begin.

Perhaps the delegation sent by the senators
to meet the Vandals outside the gates,
the Pope and his entourage at its head,
perhaps His Grace, magnificent in a mitre
and crosier in hand, would remind the Vandals
that they after all were Christians like him
and persuade them to return to Africa.

It's then you'll observe, with unusual attention,
the small brown sparrow that hops in the yard
wholly oblivious to your pressing concerns,
and, pondering a while the works of the Stoics,
will reach the reasoned if troubling conclusion
that a whiff of incense, a bishop's raised hand
were unlikely to expiate the hunger for possessions,
the self-righteous wrath of peasant soldiers
drawn up in sight of the riches of a Rome
that year after year had made them feel
so excluded from power, so worthless, so dumb.

There comes at last what you've always dreaded,
the sound of chanting coming down the street,
the smash of a sledgehammer breaking a door,
a threnody of pleading, of wailing, a scream.

You lower your head, embrace your knees,
and hope, in a quietly mesmerised way,
the Vandals will never find out where you are.

An Argument in Utica

~ north coast of Africa, circa 630 BCE

Don't ever trust Phoenicians, my child, my mother said,
her fingers reddened by the entrails of the scrublands goat
she sat and skinned with me outside the kitchen door.

But what about those friends of yours from Tyre? I asked.
Nobody trusts their smiles and money-lending talk at all.
Exceptions prove the rule, she said, and spat hard in the dust.

I knew she knew, grandma. The-one-who-can't-be-named
was back in town, curly brown beard and strong white legs,
from Tyre as well, and heir to all his uncle's leatherworks.

He'd scratch black marks like flies on a papyrus sheet
each time I dragged a pile of stiff old hides down to the quay,
then slip me bracelets, coins, a string of blue glass beads.

Phoenicians aren't all the same, I said, *besides, these days,*
there're also traders from Cadiz and Athens in the streets.
Seaside cities, they're the future, mother, just imagine

the plays, the statues, the jewellery stalls! And wasn't Utica
a dreary swamp of mud and crabs and gulls without a name
before the first Phoenician prow slid through the reeds?

She gave a shrug, grandma, and said nothing – nothing!
We worked in silence then, red meat, the fat and bones
in heaps to sell, the bowels still warm, too slippery to hold.

I saw, down in the bay, beyond the waves and fishing boats,
the wet flash of a warship's oars that rose in level rows,
rising, falling, gliding the hull towards the harbour mouth.

I felt so worried then, grandma, so worried and so scared,
remembering the riots in town, the promises he made,
the scent of cedar planks inside his uncle's slipway shed.

Kahin, mother kept saying, *you must listen to the afterlife.*
It's time, my girl, for you to go with me and sleep a night
among the burial mounds, before you lose your head.

Oh, please don't chase the fireflies of foreign charms
that twinkle in your path – they'll dance you on and on
until you're lost and floundering across a bog of pain.

I knew the remedy – scrub and hillocks, a milk-white moon,
my mother twitching as she lay among dim clumps of trees,
the incense, hymns, the She-god in a cleft of rock at dawn,

the talisman tied round my wrist, the oil rubbed on my lids,
the masked priestess, the prayers to the Womb-of-Wombs,
when all I really wished to do was stroll in town with friends.

Damn it, damn it, damn it! Next thing, I heard a gust of oaths,
and then a thong-tied pouch, hurled from the hillside path,
flew past the pomegranate tree, then slithered past the fire

towards the horns, the brindled skin and ribcage of the goat.
A blast of wrath lurched past the hens, an uncle from the south,
with Ziriot, his scarred old hunting dog, limping at his heels.

Mountains of firewood, cartloads of hay, the best of my lambs
for this, just this? he roared, and hurled his jerkin at the pouch.
My mother sighed. Each market day he'd stagger up the hill,

his face an open wound of rage, confusion, and mistrust,
and vow he'd never trade with *trickster foreigners* again –
as if we could return to desert ways, to pack donkeys and tents.

Enough of that, Gwafa, my mother said, *you burn my ears.*
You'll always feel done down until you've learnt to count,
and stop poisoning your head with their horrible cheap wine!

Yes, eat, then go and sleep, I said, *the bean pot's by the fire.*
He turned and glaring said, *A whore like you would sell*
the last ewe of the family flock to buy a string of beads.

He hit me with his stick, here, on my back then lurched away,
yes here, and here, that's why I need your help, grandma.
Aren't we just clods to foreigners? Why can't I talk to them

about fresh water sparkling down stone furrows into town,
not seeping from a trampled ooze a long, long walk away?
And marble floors, not mud where fleas and scorpions lurk?

Why can't I learn, yes, learn, this thing he calls the alphabet?
Please help, grandma! No one knows when father will return,
we think he's found a job, one of the copper mines in Crete,

and Gwafa leers at me and says, *Soft-spine, obey the ancestors!*
Did you not smell last night the greasy smell of roasting flesh?
Don't all Phoenicians burn a little one to feed their hungry god?

Dispossessing the Britons

~ Fragments on waxed wooden tablets probably written in 93 CE
by Julia (daughter of Agricola the general/ wife of Tacitus the historian)

Artefact Codex 2374.1

Julia to Tacitus in Rome: greetings.

Please hurry back,
he worsens every day.
Last night he lay awake for hours,
clutching my hand
if I stood up to leave.

He kept on telling me things
we hadn't heard before,
blurted out and left in disarray
like shards of that Etruscan vase of his,
scattered across the floor.

I've done the best I can
to sweep them up
and piece the bits together.

Candidus greets you,
he's offered us a slave, a cook from Gaul.

Claudia's learnt to count to ten,
and has a little gift for you.

Farewell, my dearest one.

May there be no ravens in the skies
to thwart your swift return.

Artefact Codex 2374.2

'Keeps coming back,' he said,
'I'm up on a ridge, rocks, trees,
helmets, horses, creaking leather,
rebel army in the valley below.

'But no, wait – before I forget,
Festus owes us money. A lot.
Write to his steward in Mantua.
Ask for the figures. Don't back off.

'Anyway – mist, early morning mist,
drifting over green meadows below.
Come on – you can put this better,
war roughens a soldier's speech.'

'What about this?' I asked.
When I read out my poem,
he reached out for my hand,
nodded, then gave a smile.

At dawn, bronze-breastplated Jupiter,
Who'd hurried north to guide Rome's fate that day,
Concealed himself inside a wraith of mist
That drifted over British farms and fields.

Artefact Codex 2374.3

'Calgacus, so I was informed,
in private, by one of our friends,
leapt on a cart, sword in hand,
and started to work up his men.

'But don't trust informers. Ever.
Tell Tacitus. After they've gone,
ponder the mind behind the mosaic,
the bag of silver hid in the hay.

'"Freedom!" he yelled, "Today at last
our Britain will once more be free!"
At which the crowd beside the barn
shouted and chanted songs of war.

'"Slavery," he said, "isn't our way.
Must we forever allow our people
to be torn off from their ancestors
and sent in chains to other lands?

'"Day after day, insulted, whipped,
our kin are exhausted by the toil
of draining marshes, felling woods,
building roads and hewing mines.

'"Who for? I ask. Weevils in Rome?
For treacherous chieftains in our midst,
snickering on about learning Latin
while selling land, and feeding their forts?

'"Does paying their tax, their corn levies
bring any release? Thieves of the world,
the Romans give the name of empire
to slaughter, looting and slavery.

'"When they've laid waste a countryside,
have burnt the farms and villages
and butchered all who dared resist,
they call that devastation peace.

'"The Druids, by prayer and sacrifice,
have raised a wall around each soul.
Each man who bravely fights today
will surely enter heaven unharmed."'

Artefact Codex 2374.9

Agricola, last night, coughing,
a towel steaming on his chest.
'Get this down,' he says, talks,
coughs, then slumps, eyes shut.

'Where was I? It's all too much now.
I can't explain. Where's the bleeder,
the Greek one? My temples, *aaah!*
Feel here, the vein keeps throbbing.

'The meadow, later, a ghastly sight.
Corpses, spears, helmets everywhere.
Dead eyes still staring, twisted bodies
groaning on grass smeared with blood.

'A few survivors wandered, aimlessly,
bending speechless over the wounded,
standing in groups, then separating,
while women wailed over their dead.

'Next day, the valley was forsaken.
The silence of desolation reigned.
Far off, above the hills of Britain rose
the smoke of farms and villages on fire.'

Saying Goodbye to the Romans

I

The day the Romans left,
they marched their standards to the ships
drawn up along a southern shore.

A crowd soon gathered on the beach
and cursed them as they passed,
some hotheads daubed their cheeks
with streaks of purple dye,
looted the mead brewed in the feasting halls
and hanged a few collaborators in the woods.

That was, I suppose, to be expected,
after so many years of Roman oppression;
it could have been worse, much worse.

It was so exhilarating to be free!

No longer paying tax to foreigners,
powerless to stop the worst of their merchants
enticing young girls behind the haystacks
with figs from Syria and wine from Gaul,
no longer fearful of their swaggering troops
torturing the dissidents in the forts
before the new proconsul did his rounds
and told them to lay off the beatings for a while,
and no more cringing
in front of engineers and magistrates
who'd take such pleasure, such jovial pleasure,

in asking how many of us could read or write
or build a level road before they came.

As if our worth as a people
could ever be judged by such things!

Good riddance to their arrogance I say.
Were we not happier, and more considerate,
before the Romans came?

II

But now there's work, much work to be done,
bypassing their tariffs on wheat and tin,
placing our people in the new institutions,
curbing the inrush of bordering clans
and luring tutors, from Rome and Greece,
to teach our youth their baffling tongue,
their tricks of governance and money lore.

Panes of glass in the turf-roofed hovels
of serf and bondsman in every dale!

I go to bed exhilarated, but ill at ease.
How can we persuade the Picts and Celts
there's no going back to the tribe?
How can we stop the wild young zealots
attacking the villas of Romans who've stayed
and want to help us build this thing they call a state?

III

And so, in a way, I've begun to miss them;
despite the cold abstractions of their speech
and their insufferable belief, that to advance
we'd have to take Rome into our hearts,
I have, from time to time, begun to miss them.

How can you, Ethelbert? my agemates ask.

The throng of serfs, scythes in hand,
hanging around the gate of my farm all day,
that's why, I say, *that's why*.

Have you not also heard them complain
of unworked fields and empty barns,
of bribes extracted by petty officials,
posts restricted to certain bloodlines
and a knife in the back for those who protest?

And now, ha – even the Druids!

When they rip mistletoe from the trees
and shaking fists, harangue unlettered folk
about the loose behaviour in the villages
and the mad expectation burning the youth
that life should get better with every year,
I miss, in a way, an old if bitter consolation.

I miss being able to shrug and say,
Not us, not us, the Romans are to blame.

Notes

Page xii and 5

Inkosazana yeZulu is isiZulu for Princess of the Heavens.

Page 46

The Vandal army entered Rome on the 2nd of June 455 CE

Acknowledgements

Thanks are due to the editors of the following publishers and journals in whose pages versions of some of these poems first appeared: *Akroterion*, Bateleur Press, David Philip Publishers, *English Academy Review*, *Contrast*, Grocott's Mail, *Il Tolomeo*, *Literator*, *Le Simple Gadi*, New Africa Books, *New Contrast*, *Scrutiny2*, *Stanzas*, Comrades Marathon Association, *Oxford Magazine*, *The Spire* and UKZN Press.

Chris Mann

Michael Lambert Biography

Michael Lambert was Senior Lecturer in Classics at the University of KwaZulu-Natal (Pietermaritzburg), where he taught Greek, Latin, Classical Civilization, Spanish and Gender Studies (1980–2012). Since retirement, he has lectured at UCT and at Rhodes University, where he is currently a Research Associate in the School of Languages and Literatures. Author of *The Classics and South African Identities* (Bloomsbury/Bristol Classical Press, 2011), he has also published work on comparative ancient Greek and traditional Zulu ritual, on gender and sexuality in antiquity, and on Greek and Latin literature. Former chairperson of the Classical Association of South Africa, he has represented CASA at FIEC, the international federation of classical associations. A regular contributor of papers at conferences, locally and abroad (e.g. USA, Canada, Germany, Spain and Greece), he has also delivered the Leventis lecture at the University of Ibadan in Nigeria. He directed the University Madrigal Singers at UKZN for more than 30 years and has led many tours to Greece, Italy, Turkey, Egypt, Jordan, Israel and China. He has also performed poetry in English, Greek and Latin at arts festivals in Grahamstown and Hilton, and has been a regular speaker at French Week symposia and functions since the inception of the French Presence in KZN project.

OTHER WORKS IN THE DRYAD PRESS LIVING POETS SERIES

AVAILABLE NOW

Transcontinental Delay, Simon van Schalkwyk
The Mountain Behind the House, Kobus Moolman
In Praise of Hotel Rooms, Fiona Zerbst
catalien, Oliver Findlay Price
Allegories of the Everyday, Brian Walter
Otherwise Occupied, Sally Ann Murray
Landscapes of Light and Loss, Stephen Symons
An Unobtrusive Vice, Tony Ullyatt
A Private Audience, Beverly Rycroft
Metaphysical Balm, Michèle Betty

FORTHCOMING IN 2021

Dark Horse, Michèle Betty

OTHER WORKS BY DRYAD PRESS (PTY) LTD

River Willows: Senryū from Lockdown, Tony Ullyatt
missing, Beverly Rycroft
The Coroner's Wife: Poems in Translation, Joan Hambidge
Unearthed: A Selection of the Best Poems of 2016, edited by Joan Hambidge
and Michèle Betty

Available in South Africa online at www.dryadpress.co.za
from better bookstores and internationally from African Books Collective
(www.africanbookscollective.com)